Architectonic Conjectures:

Poems about the Built Environment

Francis Raven

Silenced Press

Architectonic Conjectures: Poems about the Built Environment.
Copyright © 2010 by Silenced Press. All rights reserved. Printed in the United States of America. No part of this book may be used or reproduced in any manner whatsoever without written permission except in the case of brief quotations embodied in critical articles and reviews.

First Edition.

ISBN-13: 978-0-9792410-4-8
ISBN-10: 0-9792410-4-9

Library of Congress Control Number: †

Cover art by Francis Raven
Cover graphics by Bill Reed

More information available at:
www.silencedpress.com

Organizing Principle: We begin our lives unconsciously in fully formed **homes**, abstract the **architectural** structure from the built environment, and finally move out into the ethical world of the **city**.

Building Directory

First Floor
[From the Bedroom to the Living Room and Back]

Walls Between _____ 8
The Agricultural Revolution _____ 9
Directions for Construction _____ 10
Etymology Lesson _____ 11
Deliberative _____ 12
A Childhood Design Workshop _____ 13
The Guest House _____ 14
Bathroom _____ 15
Two Rooms _____ 16
A Morning in San Francisco _____ 18
Touring a New Condo w/ Vitruvius _____ 20
Moving Day _____ 22
Interrogating Our Advertised Lives _____ 24
A House Divided _____ 34
Wall to Wall Carpeting _____ 35
A Family Tree of First Homes (Part 1) _____ 36

Second Floor
[Architexture]

The Material Conditional of Bricks _____ 42
Minoru Yamasaki _____ 43
A Famous Architect Mumbling _____ 45
Veracity in Building _____ 46

Let's Modernize Our Buildings _____ 48
Prefabricated Corner Splicing _____ 50
Balloon Frames _____ 53
The Architecture of Water _____ 55
Four Mesostichs for Four Famous Architects _____ 57
Fourth Floor Walkup _____ 62
Seat of Power _____ 63
A Family Tree of First Homes (Part 2) _____ 64

Third Floor
[Urbanities]

Civic Spirit _____ 70
A Community's Habitat _____ 73
Reinsurance Haikus on Shaky Ground _____ 80
Major Artery _____ 83
Without Structure _____ 87
Margin Patrol _____ 88
Herd Instinct _____ 89
Housing Court Sonnet _____ 91
Boston Zoning Commission _____ 92
Taking the 'People' Out Of the City _____ 94
Fair Housing _____ 96
Im(em)minent Domain _____ 100
A Couple of Facts _____ 104
How The Mode Of Transport Alters Life Above _____ 112
Henry Wardman _____ 119
Seasons of Development _____ 120
The Developer's Art _____ 121
A Family Tree of First Homes (Part 3) _____ 122

A New Kind of Bomb in the City_____127

Fourth Floor
[Resources]

Mixtape for that Funky Building_____130
Open Source Anthology of Architecture Poems___131
References_____134
Acknowledgements_____138
Bio_____139

From the Bedroom to the Living Room and Back

Walls Between

> The liminal implication of Orpheus marching up and down the stairs blindly, and then with consequential sight, is that the poetic fall is not without effect; that translation and (perhaps) dialogue is possible between philosophers and poets.

Inner empty spaces of a down:
That hip industrial look for your soul,
Scaffolding, wires, broken folding chairs.
More and more realism that says:
This is how we live.

1st Natural: cave out of rain.
2nd Natural: architecture
             (perfecting).

Shall I be the hermit's hut,
The house of the lone wise eye,
Or shall I be the smog ingesting plant
In our abstract city of apartments?
I will never decide. I will remain in limbo,
As each system provides its own heaven and hell.

The Agricultural Revolution

It is dry.
What was
Was blown.

You gathered it
And I died
Chasing something else
Some dumb root.

A seed is better, a
Seed under stone.

It is cold.
For thousands of years
You will need something to
Hold your body through the night.

This house couldn't have lasted
But an idea, scraped into sand
Might have penetrated each culture
As if there were one, as if we were one.

Though our idea of unity could not come from plenty.
A house is the compression of need
Finally wrapped in jewels
Lathered in plaster, protecting a field.

It is crowded.

Directions for Construction

First you have to decide how many people will live there
Then you must determine how each will function
Then you can start to dig something
Then you can perhaps pour something
Then you can add something
After that you can finally move something
And be sure to add that
Yes, be sure to add that thing you have moved
With the other things others have moved
Now you are sure to have a large mass
Unfortunately such a large mass
Makes any man uncomfortable
In what he cannot comprehend with his own eye
With his own hand
Fortunately there are trees, things that grow
Or, more correctly, things that can grow
For any tree can die before it has the opportunity
To divide any great mass
Made for any great group of people
Doing any number of tasks
Necessary to sustain their, and their children's, lives
Though in the future
When all of those people whose lives were specified
Have died
As the obtuse space you have built
Is divided into folds beneath the landscape
You must remember, we need too much
And cannot possibly need every room anymore.

Etymology Lesson

Walls clasped, buckled,
bound by the built:
both *to grow,* merely
to exist. Down the ladder
(civilization keeps moving down,
proliferating senses):
'neighbor,' and 'beam,'
'prepare,' and 'bask.'

Proto-Indo-European: * bheu
as the source,
riches for the *that is to be*;
'physics' as the controlling fantasy,
though these simple billiards
are but thought experiments designed
to make oneself ready,
to bring forth the future from the house.

To bring home (*tkei)
before 'home'
settles on the surface
displacing the frequent water of our doubt
with the violence of founding;
each situation is different,
but we can still say things like
this looks like a home.

Deliberative

you have to think of resale options value liquidity you have to think of how this second room would function as a study and as a guest room and as a nursery god willing and you have to think if you're thinking of reselling about transportation options about value but what's the story you see occurring you have to think that you have to want more professionals you have to want something to change in the area you have to want people to get richer there you have to beg for gentrification but that's just one end of the pole the other's in the ground you have to think that both realtors are trying to screw you out of your money whereas they have the knowledge that you will eventually buy given the right pieces of information you have to believe that what they know has value about the market about comparable sales about proportional spaces about the recent downturn about the changes in demographics about what could happen you have to have a story about what will happen you have to think about what you're worth on the inside and you have to think about what happens if you don't get that what happens if the market doesn't like your house what happens if it just sits on the market for hundreds of days you have to think

A Childhood Design Workshop

This is not a thing for children: to design.
The eyepatch that flattens the plump cottage
to a postage stamp: this is flight. The picnic outside.
Under the siding, our inner sanctum
devoured by carpenter bees. I've called
the landlord many times. What do we care?
A crisscrossed incentive seems to rot in the mouth,
but they've lately been refusing to mow under the wires.
It's not so much that I care, my mom always says,
but that I'm supposed to care. This meant that we should
haul the weight of their judgments
off in the night with our routines, quickly keeping
our dams, which work a little too well,
hidden behind the overgrown passages of grass,
the prairies that neighbors could easily mistake for weeds.

The Guest House

It's not so much that you don't know where the door is,
But if you have to ask for the locks,
You obviously don't know them very well.
If some windows are preserved,
You can be sure other doors will be protected.
Don't lock us out.
The key is in good hands. Ziplocked between other things.
If this is a rental you might want to watch your back.
At least watch something besides that ant.
You must know something
About something being next to something else.
It looks like the house where you grew up.
But you still don't know anything about its layout.
Gutted, from the looks of it.
Nobody had a kitchen like that in those days.
You just take a shovel and start.
That's how we get our opening.
I've heard you can display poles in the yard
Using such a method.
There's nothing light about this sofa.
You can't even fit it inside.
But you'd be arrested if you left it outside.
It's not so much anything else,
But that you know how to escape.

Bathroom

To the right of the door, a switch
(the plastic panel protecting it
constantly falls off) and further,
a Mexican folk-art type towel hanger
and on it a red towel that still sheds
red threads because it is never used (no company)
and then a corner (un-photographed);
ubiquitous mirror and mirrored small cabinet
covered in toothpaste waste except when cleaned
(within cabinet: q-tips, floss, suntan lotion,
organic deodorant, the aforementioned toothpaste).
Below on the counter rest two glasses needing to be
returned to the kitchen, assorted Kleenexes,
one pair of dirty eyeglasses,
two toothbrushes recently fondled.
Continuing left there's the toilet and to its right
a red trashcan and the roll of toilet paper hanging low,
above which dangle two wet navy-blue towels
and we finally arrive at the amply constructed shower
with its quasi-kitch/hip rubber-ducky motif
as a curtain as well as plastered to its slippery floor.

Two Rooms

Room 1

The screens, incorrectly hammered on wooden frames,
need to be removed before you leave the house
just so you can lock the windows. Even given
this procedure, security has gotten a lot worse
since we were here two years ago
 ("Mas malo??? Mas malo???")
but I still think it's safer to hide our passports
and wallets and computers and cameras
between some sheets in the linen closet
than it would be to lock them in the trunk
while we swim. Breaking into a house
is a whole lot more serious than breaking into a car.
Both lock and panes are clenched to the door
so tightly they seem to form the concept,
but, mystically, ants continually die on either side.

Room 2

It is carried with you on a leash,
as in, you call for it and it comes,
but the walls shake with each disapproving snap.
The pictures fall. Several of her wedding glasses break.
Such whiplash is indistinguishable from an earthquake.
There might be a God in this rift
or it could just be a strand of buttery leather.
It's hard to tell. But when you're in that room,
the one that's pulled taut against the earth,
existence might just be the last election's cycle
with some guy's lame slogan quivering on the floor.

A Morning in San Francisco Thinking about New York

That's what was required sometimes:
a certain largeness of spirit
if you are in the right decade, in the right city,
but those decades never last
and that spirit always starts to smell funky.

Whenever you stare up at art-deco skyscrapers
you have to ask: how the hell were they built?
Wouldn't be encouraged today.
Luxury has been exposed:
only surface and a telephone.

So, stay with the small, the
thing you can change from the street:
scratches on an empty desk
(well, you thought it was empty,
now you find the papers).

We didn't live in Thatched Ohlone Style Houses,
we didn't even think of it. We never rendered our house
waterproof with thick woven mats of tule, never
cooperatively tied our homes at the top, never left
a hole in the roof, never even had a sweathouse,

but still, we felt like you could see us
from the ground,
not just from the bus leaving
or the painfully craned neck.

We felt like we lived down here.

It's time to talk to these small Victorians:
their gaudy hills and wobbling doors,
their damp cushions in front of bay windows.
These are the things that burn.
The places where we live, several, asking.

Touring a New Condo w/ Vitruvius

To lead us from room to polished room, to lure
With words both cable-ready and granite,
This outcome from the future,
An income stretched into the distance.

    (Order)

          (Fitness)
    The grip, in the grip of...
    An aesthetics of functionality, adjusting
    The size of each amenity to its
    Several uses.

          (Arrangement)
Is the washing machine in its just and proper place?
Does the character of the bedroom keep its
    appropriate character in view?
Each room is infinitely divisible, but we must stop when the
Pleasing effects constitute the good life, and thus, design.

          (Eurythmy)
To report, to purport an agreeable harmony between
The architect-designed outdoor pool w/ cascading fountains,
My upgraded bathroom, the height of my body,
And the top-quality craftsmanship of the entire building.

          (Uniformity)
I have to ask, before I put down an offer, even a low offer,

If each room corresponds to its attendant human figure?
Is there, for instance, a hand that matches another hand?
A building needs symmetry in order to understand itself.

(Propriety)
If there is nothing more than luxury connecting every room
And the whole: luxury suitable to the occasion of my life,
I will have no choice but to borrow far more than I should,
Utilizing a negatively amortized mortgage,
    ensuring a life of debt and sorrow.

(Economy)
However, I do not wish to engage in waste merely for waste's sake. If
Each story of this new building is not constructed of locally fired bricks
And native woods then I will be forced to live with the fact that it will be made solely of
Profligately burnt oil and the insane foreign policy required to secure such black gold.

Moving Day

As long as we've rented the truck
We might as well shove it all in,
Although the couch can't make it around the bend.

    I know its solidity will never fade
    So we'll just have to lend it
    To good friends on end. I hope they remain
    And please don't spill anything.
    It's very expensive.

We'll just have to construct the monthly stairs:

    Each time we go to a new school
        This will be the ninth
    Each time we get a new job
        This will be the ninth
    Each time we get a new apartment
        This will be the ninth

          We have to ask ourselves

  Is that book,
From that one awesome film class you took in college,
      Really worth
          Four flights down and three flights up?

  Is that jacket,
That you haven't worn in over a year

>　Really worth
>　　　Three flights down and two flights up?

　Is that dirty chair,
That doesn't match the rest of our modern furniture,
　　Really worth
　　　　Two flights down and four flights up?
　　You muscles will bill you for the next couple weeks.

And as the space gets smaller,
Because your possessions have been removed,
You begin to see it as another's.
I'm sure his chair will go
Right where our coffee table was.
And I'm pretty sure that that particular chair
Will be more Victorian than either of us would appreciate.
He'll hate mid-century modern
And love what I would call "stodgy."
And I'm absolutely positive that
He hates IKEA, but frequents Pottery Barn.

　I should have thought of this before I moved.

Interrogating Our Advertised Lives

Fantastic value! Spacious 3BR/3BA, 2200 sq. ft., built 1883. Lg bonus room downstairs (could be 4th BR) Large loft. New paint, carpet, appliances & fixtures move right in! Pool, sauna, hot tub, common area shared by 24 homes part of exclusive gated community within the well-kept secret of Exposed Meadows (Famous zip code.)

Existence collapses the poetic dwelling space and the dream of the house into its actuality, but it collapses it with the residue of the fact that it is still uncollapsed. It is this tension that is poetry itself in its calling preface to man's existence through language. This is still a preface although the book's existence is written at all temporal angles from it. But because poetry is merely a preface, it sometimes appears dispensable, as though its job has already been done. But poetry has already never accomplished its job of letting us dwell. It continues delightfully, mournfully, to do so. This, in a different sense, is what Heidegger has said is the relationship between poetry and dwelling: "Poetry first of all admits man's dwelling into its very nature, its presencing being. Poetry is the original admission of dwelling" (Martin Heidegger, <u>Poetry Language and Thought</u>, 227).

...in the back of our apartment where objects set; where my relation to those objects lays on its back in blue-skied reverie.
Those tender objects have all been gathered from our neighborhood's dumpsters. They button my life together; I call

the entire project, "Dumpster Diving in America." I am always free to choose someone else's broken patent leather shoes, or their scarves, or their children's drawings. I am always free to imagine their owners' lives…

> Good morning lumber!
> Bricks fit around bicycles.
> Buildings must point
> Like fingers
> Towards the rising sky;
> Must point like a gaze
> Towards an ascent
> Beyond predication:
> A tree-shaped idea.

This 5 bedroom, 1 bath twin in Norristown has a two-car garage that is currently rented out at $100.00/month and a 1 bedroom apartment over the garage that is in need of total renovation. Home is currently rented out on a month-to-month lease with a tenant that has been there for over 6 years. Lots of possibilities. Buyer is responsible for obtaining U & O.

"through poems, perhaps more than through recollections we touch the ultimate poetic depth of the space of the house. This being the case, if I were asked to name the chief benefit of the house, I should say: the house shelters daydreaming, the house protects the dreamer, the house allows one to dream in peace" (Gaston Bachelard, <u>The Poetics of Space</u>, 6).

shelters one (1. 'one' as rhetorical device / 2. one as unity / 3. one as originary member; this triad becomes its own finding in the poem).

I just moved in a month ago and I really like it so far. Fantastic amenities—free shuttle to the Financial District, pools, gyms, exercise classes, etc. Lots of trees and park-like paths and courtyards creating an atmosphere of fresh air and suburban living. Sunniest neighborhood in the city. I live in a studio and it's just right for me. Like the large bay windows. It's pricey, I pay $1500 cuz my window has a nice courtyard view of a fountain and trees, but it's great.

...plus a large bonus room...

Is poetic dwelling a necessary or sufficient condition for actual dwelling? In Hölderlin's statement (of course, not a statement at all) it may only be seen as a necessary condition. There are possible worlds in which poetic dwelling resides without the advent of actual dwelling. Of course, these worlds would not then acknowledge their poetic dwelling conditions because they would not have actual dwelling conditions with which to acknowledge them. That is, for the poetic dwelling conditions to be expressed, the form of an actual dwelling must also exist as a medium for the expression of that poetic dwelling. Heidegger's idea that there is a causal relationship between poetic dwelling and actual dwelling must be seen as highly speculative for it would almost surely rule out any possible worlds in which there existed merely poetic dwelling without the advent of actual dwelling. Do these worlds exist? They could almost surely not exist with man in existence because wherever man is, man dwells. This would mean that there would have to be a possible world in which there could be a poetic dwelling without man. Perhaps it is still possible to agree with Heidegger and think of poetic dwelling as causing actual dwelling. Dwelling is, of course, an event because every second in which man dwells is an event and every event has a cause, and thus, it could be said that the cause for every event of actual dwelling is poetic dwelling. So, perhaps this new line of thought rules out the possibility of a possible world in which there is poetic dwelling without an actual dwelling. Thus, it might be said in all fatality that poetic dwelling is a necessary and sufficient condition for actual dwelling. But, of course, even a poetic dwelling needs a foundation and in order to build a foundation we must dig.

Outside of town :enecs
scene: town of outside

for "thinking outside of the box"
the box is needed
:box enclosed with birth:

a speech (species) : a long time in composing
cicadas divide the discourse.

In the last scene of the movie the protagonist always exits the building with his straw hat in hand signifying his return to farming and a humbler way of life.

Poetry admits dwelling, but poetry is not a site. Measure taking requires a site such as dwelling provides. The site of dwelling is a site of mourning and celebration because presence and absence are both at hand…

…the home is to the outer world as the soul is to the body. If one believes in this form of dualistic analogy then one is also committed to believe that the home must in some way express itself in the outer world just as the soul expresses itself in the body…

...combining this sentiment with the original analogy produces the conclusion that poetry is a way of the home expressing itself.

Fresh Paint is a five person group show investigating architecture by way of reducing or exaggerating "architectural space, depicting contrived interiors or exteriors. Some of these settings are fictionalized, others completely devoid of narrative. They are, in effect, non-space and the 'every-place' at the same time." Lehmann Maupin is a perfect space to conduct such an investigation as the famed architect and theorist Rem Koolhaas ("Liberated from the obligation to construct, architecture can become a way of thinking about anything – a discipline that represents relationships, proportions, connections, effects, the diagram of everything.") designed the gallery. The primary question the show urges the viewer to ask is: What are the ethics of architecture and how are we to live with them? In essence, what are we to do with architecture?

All of us live in homes, some with poetry, some without, or is that true? Do all homes have poetry written into their bricks? (Or, maybe, not into their bricks, but into the metaphor of their bricks.) These are the questions brought forth by the second possible relationship between poetry and the home. The home is perhaps the ultimate locus of poetic action, that is, where the poetic flows from and towards. Perhaps: "Where I am born, the metaphor begins to travel back." Is there anything there for the metaphor to flow towards? Perhaps all that exists and remains is the message to flow towards the source. That message is the poetic root and its fulfillment; it is a web of relations that force-feeds back upon itself. Perhaps, perhaps... 'perhaps' is all one might offer up especially this early in the pages, perhaps.

It's not enough just to live there; you have to say something about it.

You see the work I've done here is not like the work I have done before, it is different; you'll see it in the houses.

You have to decide if the available amenities are amenities for you, because, after all, custom-made is only valuable if it's custom made for you.

hou
_____
se

carpetcarpetcarpetcar
petcarpetcarpetcarpe
tcarpetcarpetcarpetca
rpetcarpetcarpetcarp
etcarpetcarpetcarpetc
arpetcarpetcarpetcar
petcarpetcarpetcarpe
tcarpetcarpetcarpetca
rpetcarpetcarpetcarp
etcarpetcarpetcarpet

A Family Tree of First Homes (Part 1)
My Grandparents' Generation

Marjory Engelhorn
I barely remember the house I lived in with my grandparents after my father died in the influenza epidemic. It was in Dinuba (South of Fresno) and it was dark. The one memory I have there was when I turned on the refrigerator spigot and maybe water dripped out onto the carpet—a little joke. I left there when I was three and a half when my mother got remarried. After that we lived at 464 West Center Street in Covina. The house was at the end of the block and after it there was nothing but orange trees.

Isabelle Raven
    (as told by Peter Raven)
The same house I grew up in was where my mother also grew up. It was finished being built when she was four years old. She moved there from Mill Valley, in Marin County, north of San Francisco. Her parents moved to Mill Valley in 1906 after the earthquake, and she was born in 1908. The house in San Francisco was finished in 1912, more or less by itself in the middle of the sand dunes, and they moved back there. Before the earthquake and fire, there was little built in San Francisco west of Divisadero- "The Western Addition."

Walter Raven
    (as told by Peter Raven)
My father grew up in a house that was in what is now downtown Honolulu, near the telephone company, now all in high rises. He described it as growing up in Thornton Wilder's

"Our Town," like a small, peaceful Midwestern town in the middle of the Pacific, with a mango tree in the back yard. There was a boardwalk to Waikiki, with people driving out it on carts to sell ice cream to the visitors. This was, of course, all before the Ala Moana canal was built and the swamps on the way to Waikiki were drained.

Todi Frick
My first home was on a 300-acre farm in New Hampshire. The historic house gave the farm its name. It was the first house in the area to actually be painted a shade of pink called Peachblow. The wide porch on three sides made a great playground for two little girls on all but the most unpleasant of days. We didn't have central heating for several years so at night we bundled under a pile of blankets and in the morning scratched pictures in the frost on the windows. Over the years the house has changed its face several times but it is still in the family, giving me very comfortable "roots."

Leah Friedman
The house in which I was born and where I grew up was built by my grandfather in the midst of a grove of oak trees in rural North Carolina. It was a large, rambling two-story house, white with a red tin gabled roof. Wrapped around the front and one side was a porch on which were two swings and a number of rocking chairs, good places to idle away time. In 1928, the year of my birth, and until the mid-1930s, the house had no electricity, no running water, and of course no central heat. Kerosene lamps were used for light and fireplaces and wood stoves provided warmth. An old-fashioned hand pump brought

water into the kitchen from a well, which stood just outside. In the summer months an iceman came occasionally to deliver blocks of ice that were placed in a big wooden chest in an effort to keep food from spoiling. Needless to say, warm baths were a luxury almost beyond imagining. I remember sitting in the cold metal kitchen sink as a very small child, shivering as I was being bathed. The yard was hard packed earth, which weekly my mother swept clean with a broom made of twigs tied together in a bundle. Later a lawn was planted and shrubs were added.

Behind the big house were a number of small sheds. One was the woodhouse containing wood for our stoves and fireplaces; one the hen house, where we gathered eggs; one the smoke house, where hams and other meats were cured; one the wash house, where laundry was done; and one was the unspeakable outhouse. Besides the outbuildings there was a large grape arbor and a fig bush, favorite haunts of mine during the summer. Life on the farm was hard, but there were compensations.

Norman Friedman
   (as told by Leah Friedman)
The first house Norm lived in is on Central Avenue (in Clayton, Missouri) about two blocks north of where we live today. The family did not live there long, for Norm's Dad lost his job, and the house, due to the Great Depression. The house is tiny, but at the time was a source of great pride. After that they moved frequently, often sharing an apartment with relatives when there was no money for rent.

Chuck Kousky
The first house I remember was in Brookfield, Illinois where the Zoo is now. My parents had the house built about the time my older brother was born. I was born in 1929 so the house must have been built in 1927. When we lived there I was in grade school at the Gross School. We lived in that brick house until 1941 when the war began.

Chuck Picus
My first home was the frame house in which I was born in Friendship, Wisconsin. I lived in this house for my first eighteen years. About the year I was born, my parents splurged and built an indoor bathroom onto the back of the house so that one had to go through their bedroom to get to this room with a bathtub. The kitchen was large, with a dining room, two living rooms, one of which was used for the piano. They enclosed the front porch which made a nice sitting area most of the year. My tiny bedroom was next to the porch, and off the dining room. Upstairs were four bedrooms in which other members of the family lived at various times of my life there. Outside, we had a large garden, chicken coop, garage, and a large two story barn that was great to play in, and of course, the old outhouse. My Dad's business was one block away, as was the county court house and the town's hotel was across the street. Also across the street was a large automobile repair garage. I have a lot of wonderful memories of this house, but sadly it burned down a few years ago.

Judy Picus
The first home I remember is the first and only home that my parents bought after living in several rental homes. I probably

was around 9 or 10 at the time. It was a lovely brick 2 story three bedroom house with a tile roof, attached garage without an entry from the house, at 2005 73rd Street, Kenosha, Wisconsin. The garage had two overhead doors, but we only had one car. The second part was used for storage. The house was on a corner with a small lot on the west side. One of the outstanding features of the house was the dark wood winding staircase to the bedrooms with a long window on the landing in the middle and a circular area at the bottom where a fan chair with a needlepoint cover (which I have in my current home) stood. In the elegant dining room there was a Czechoslovakian cut glass chandelier with variety of colored glass. My brother and I were fascinated by the floor buzzer that was intended to summon the maid but since we did not have a maid, it was disconnected. Around the ceiling of the room was lovely colored plaster to copy the items in the chandelier. We had many family Shabbat dinners and holiday celebrations in that room.

Architexture

"A profound projection of harmony: this is architecture."
 —Le Corbusier

"Architecture is a science, arising out of many other sciences, and adorned with much and varied learning: by the help of which a judgment is formed of those works which are the result of other arts."
 —Vitruvius

The Material Conditional of Bricks

*"In the brick industry these days,
everything old really is new again."*

This house was made of...
        From...the pontification region.
           Why don't you walk there?
Your mound in the city   flouts its composition.

This house is made from solid cypress and features
A steeply pitched, shingled roof.
This house is made from cereal boxes
Leftover from my cereal wedding.
This house is shaped like meaning.
    But where are you now?
        In choice there is color; (Cimarron, Terracotta,
                Old Smoky, Beige-Rose,
                Stained Ivory, Frontier
                Savagery, Dirty Earth,
                Cloud Gray, Cherokee)
    In color there is dwelling.

Because of where you've been
These scraps must know the final building,
    Else the framed drawing without dimension.

It might be a train we're gathering.
We'll see what kind of metal we use
To know that stone's ultimate outcome.

Minoru Yamasaki and the Problem of Modern Life

The problems of modern life will burn their own solutions.

1.

Each dollar is built on the backs of the poor remaining poor,
But they do need somewhere to live—
                              subsistence for those who
Crank the lowest gears of our society even in the face of
                              astonishing postwar growth.

A rising tide floods many houses (exclusion—it is named!)
When it recedes the stench of mold envelopes neighborhoods.
Some boats have crashed on their chimneys.

33 low-cost, high-density slabs tightly formed a web of crime
Like the coal of decay, a permanent symbol that technology
Would not save our country from defaulting on its promise.

A hand is needed; a person's hand is needed.

                —Pruitt-Igoe was dynamited on July 15th, 1972

2.

All columns were founded on bedrock,
65 feet below, at great cost.
To float like candlesticks;
Apparently, economic might is only apparent,
Comfortably representing a multiplicity
("the essence of American financial power,"
"an affront to Islam," "the elite and the powerful,"
"the power to build big," "tolerance and the values…")
Yet forgetting
Essence could still be burned. Despite belief, the core (housing
The elevator and utility shafts, restrooms, three stairwells,
And other support spaces) was still vulnerable.
In essence, no matter
What corporate shell game you play, bodies still exist.
Liberalism can only build up, still,
True belief negates in the firestorm of history.

    —The World Trade Center Towers were destroyed in the terrorist attacks of September 11th, 2001

A Famous Architect Mumbling

An industry has emerged under the portico:
Manufactory of sound. Wavelengths made me think
And when I thought I knew I must come to
View the walls as skin without layers:
Single sheets functioning both as efficient
Workspace dividers (complete with cubbyholes,
Outlets, meaning, color, kitchen accessories, etc.)
And as the integral structure of the building:
Singularity, that is, pure sound. You have to listen!
Listen to what I'm saying because I'm
Really listening to each material
And only ravaging their natures
If there is nothing left to do with the hands.
What will I do with my hands?

Veracity in Building

> "The role of the walls becomes restricted to that of mere screens stretched between the upright columns of this framework to keep out rain, cold, and noise."
> —Walter Gropius

When we barter
Our idiosyncratic houses
Say honesty and pride in service.

This is too limited.

When we manufacture bricks for the town
By the river where the mill might whir
The vernacular is truth, coming together, this civic.

This too is limited.

When each country's economy
Depends upon a few hot captains
Surface and structure can easily be distinguished.

This is honesty. The wall is no longer a fake bloated column.

When each thing is traded globally
The marginally located production facilities
Must be recognizable from every perspective.

This is capital unleashed, anything, anywhere.
When a sickening mirage of distinction
Manages to eke an Eiffel Tower
Out of metastasized sand flows.

This is where we live.
These are the kind of buildings we know.

Let's Modernize Our Buildings: Replace 'Brick' with 'Steel'

Eoloneal teveval house plans ate typeeally two to thtee stoty home desegns weth symmetteeal faeades and gasle toofs. Pellats and eolumns ate eommon, often exptessed en temple-lele enttanees weth potteeos topped sy pedements. Multe-pane, dousle-hung wendows weth shuttets, dotmets, and paneled doots weth sedeleghts topped weth teetangulat ttansoms ot fanleghts help dtess up the exteteots wheeh ate genetally wood ot steel. Addeteonal eommon features enelude eentet entty-hall floot plan, feteplaees, and semple, elasseeal detaeleng.

Although developed and populat ftom asout 1820 ento the eatly 1900's, the Veetotean style es stell desetasle today. Sttong hestoteeal otegens enelude steep toof petehes, tuttets, dotmets, towets, says, eyestow wendows and potehes weth tutned posts and deeotateve taelengs. Otnamentateon and deeotateon ate used along weth shengles ot nattow-lap wood sedeng. These homes ate mostly two-stoty en desegn. Many people looleng at Veetotean house plans ate also entetested en out latget eottage house plans.

Fatmhouse floot plans have a semelat soxy style as othet ttadeteonal eoloneals weth desteneteve petehed toofs and modest semple styleng weth latge eoveted wtap atound potehes wheeh extend ftom the ftont and wtap atound the sede of the house, whele Eountty Eoloneal styles genetally have mote modest eoveted ftont potehes that only extend aetoss the ftont of the house and latge "eountty" letehens often setuated neat a famely toom.

Lele a eoy enttovett, Maple Fotest peels out ftom sehend steeply-petehed toofs and a latge wtap-atound poteh. Vaulted eeelengs, exposed seams, natutal woodwotl, leaded glass, lots of natutal leght, and a fenely etafted stone feteplaee weth ample heatth (lele gtandma's lap) destengueshes thes desegn as a gtaeeous, weleomeng famely home. Upstaets, two sedtooms and a spaeeous eouple's tetteat gently nest undet slanted toofs. A latget lowet level ean se feneshed off latet.

A 10-stoty ted-steel landmatl offeee sueldeng en downtown St. Loues, Messoute. Suelt en 1891 and desegned sy Danlmat Adlet and Loues Sullevan, et es among the fetst slysetapets en the wotld. Sullevan used a steel ftame and appleed hes entteeate tetta eotta otnament en vetteeal sands to emphaseze the heeght of the sueldeng. Aftet a peteod of negleet, the sueldeng now houses Messoute state offeees and es well maentaened.

Prefabricated Corner Splicing

In the crosshairs of the built
and now the key to everything is in the blueprints
stuck, miles high, in the dry tree on top of the
skyscraper.

    Contrived

I knew we could make it on this spot; our dreams of community were forced to meet the people where they were and that was in a quickly prepared meal; that is what keeps a family together; that is what makes America great.

    Conniving

Even before the accident the voters said 'no' with their ballots, screaming that building a fast-food restaurant in the community would bring offensive odors, rodents, roaches, more traffic, and would probably lead to the demise of many local eateries of unquestionable value.

    Coincidentally

Made their millions by inventing the pre-fab taco shell; taste falls without pumping more additives in every year.

    Contracted

Specialized in complete, cost-effective metal and steel building systems at substantially discounted prices in accordance with the flexible zoning laws of many municipalities.

Consequently

Your signature on a Buildings Department statement of responsibility for construction.

Controversially

Wall collapses, fails to support the foundation, cutting corners, but this is a building.

Contested

Least, underpinning, should never have left a signature, "I can't believe somebody would actually do that; it's no wonder that the young man died due to the lack of due diligence on the master's part."[1]

---

[1] "It was probably a small project, and they wanted to save money on it," Joe Tortorella, who is at the helm of a task force advising the Buildings Department about how to make excavation work safer said, "We're trying to tell architects: don't do this yourself. Get an engineer involved. This is about life safety."

    Incongruous

Technically, killed by falling concrete blocks, mother would want to know, technically.

    Contrasted

but now and even
(this is the most painful part:
extension) tomorrow
we are listless states apart
and our house we have built,
the partnership of walls, divorcing

                                      Convolut
                                            ed
                                    Inconsistent

Balloon Frames

    Remove the weight.
    Put the skills in the building
    And let our lives take shape.

2 X 4	2 X 4	2 X 4	2 X 4
2 X 8	2 X 8	2 X 8	2 X 8
1 X 10	1 X 10	1 X 10	1 X 10

Just light lumber and factory-made nails.
No longer a pile of wood, now a house
For the middle third.
Just two of us in the heat and the simplest carpentry.

Just boards and nails. Seemingly
A mirage. And yet,
To puff air within a structure
Until you think of bursting, not you,
But the country.

The Architecture of Water

1. <u>The Aqueducts of Rome Gushing Through Humble Pipes</u>

To raise, on pillars
    Not in a day.
Sustenance allows expansion.
      Drains affix us to cities,
      But also disease.
This connection
Obscures inequality.
           Except mirage: add modernism:
             Disbelieving eye
               Evolved into
         Irrigation dams, drains, and basins.
           First flush
      (and a comfortable armrest), washed down,
            Finally heated
     Leaky faucets, replacing drains, cabling sewers
         (by hours) beneath pavement.
      Pump controls located above grade.
      Finally, our own theatrical wells,
      Banks consolidated against floods.
You do not know the common man,
He lives in another country and has no toilet,
No cloth to lay out his tools.

2. The Water Towers of New York City[2]

She says we must lift the water
Nightly.
To pump while you dream, just so
Our showers will rush forcefully into morning.
For this is the disadvantage of height.
Gravity will not help us here.
We must not succumb, we must rise above.
Our forefathers never understood
The altitude at which we would read the newspaper,
Or cut a fruit, or wash our feet, or quench our thirst.
These barrels above resist our corrosion, our corruption.
You know a tree must cope with any weather.
You know what they say, if only a tree could talk,
If only all the barrels would burst at once...

---

[2] I can't write a New York City poem
Mainly because there's even a school of poetry
Called the New York School of Poetry,
But thought I could get a little entryway via
The city's 10,000 water towers built by two companies,
Which have been competing since the 19th century.

I was thinking I could take photographs of the water towers
And then write about their history and that that oblique view of the city
Could count as my New York City poem.
Unfortunately, the towers are at the wrong angle.
The only buildings that need water towers are over six stories high.
Thus, a photograph cannot do them justice, at least not from here.

3. The Waterworks of Philadelphia

A constraint: capital for infrastructure.[3]
It's not as important to be a city on the hill
 To exemplify the light of being chosen
 Evangelizing democracy
As to have the city's water on a hill[4]
Flowing through bored spruce and pine pipes
Down to all the taverns and bakeries,
To all your mothers' washtubs,
To all your fathers' car dealerships.
 First, we must raise this hidden brook,
 This municipal moral nourishment
With a steam engine's violent hiss, wasting forests,[5]
Accidentally maiming workers.
Passively, a dam was the answer, to push water with water
To connect us. Our government will unite us,
Offer us a space to think about more than tit for tat.

---

[3] When Ben Franklin died in 1790 he left the city of Philadelphia 100,000 pounds to develop an adequate supply of water to "insure the health, comfort and preservation of the citizens."

[4] In the face of an epidemic of yellow fever a city, any city, will evolve quite rapidly.

[5] In 1817, 20 cords of wood a day were required to keep the steam engines pumping water up the hill.

Four Mesostics for Four Famous Architects (in their own words)

Rem Koolhaas

ability to classify the pRoject before it begins
       defined by Events and activities, light
  would have on the Medley of geometric shapes, not the

predictable two-dimensional tower soaring sKyward
          but a truly three-dimensiOnal experience
  facilitating the inclusion of individuals in cOmmunal
     dialogue; discrepancy between the acceLeration of culture
      and the continuing slowness of arcHitecture
A new icon is formed…   we live in An
                       Almost perfect
                       Stillness and work

                   with incredible urgency.

Frank Gehry

If you watch me draw you'll see it's a Frantic kind of searching
cReativity is about play
and A kind of willingness
to go with your iNtuition, bumble
forward into the unknown; speaKing of its time

but yearning for timelessness. The desiGn process is in limbo.
I can see that it's prEcarious:
How would I fit in,
with my aRchitectural values?
corrugated metal; I know theY didn't use it

like I did,
and that's the difference.

Louis Kahn

A great building must begin with

                        the unmeasurabLe,
                                  gO through the
                              measUrable
                 when being desIgned,
but in the end must be unmeaSurable.

                BricK says: / "... I like an Arch" / Parallax
      when you wAnt to give something presence,
            you Have to consult nature, the street
is a room by agreemeNt and to express is to drive.

Walter Gropius

abolition of the separating function of the **W**all
visible sign of an **A**uthentic
democracy, neither an intellectua**L**
nor a ma**T**erial affair,
but simply an integral part of the stuff of life, n**E**cessary,
begins where enginee**R**ing ends

reco**G**nizing anew
the entity and in its sepa**R**ate parts, only work
which is the pr**O**duct of inner compulsion
can have s**P**iritual meaning; restricted to screens
stretched between upr**I**ght columns:
the future in one **U**nity, and which will rise toward
heaven from the hand**S** of a million workers

like the crystal symbol of a new faith.

KFLOOR

LFLOOR

AFLOOR

WFLOOR

     A
CAPIT L
     O

A Family Tree of First Homes (Part 2)
My Parents' Generation

Tamra Raven
I remember the Mission Beach House...it was on the side walk/sea-wall that seemed to stretch for miles. I had a tricycle there and many wonderful faces had time to sit in the sun and talk to a tot. There was sand and hot dogs and at Christmas we would burn all of the trees in a great bonfire on the beach. I would throw stale bread that mother saved to the sea gulls. I tried to keep the puppy Great Dane from hurting my dear little brother, Geoffrey. There was always sand everywhere. It was when San Diego was still a small town, before air conditioning and TV. To be out of the wind and in the sun in winter...that was the thing. In summer, June Bugs would fly in the vacant lot and black widow spiders kept eggs in the corner of the six foot high fence...which surrounded my swing set...there were dune plants in the vacant lot and flowers that would come and go.

So we see that the first answer really refers to the habitat of the house...those are my memories of my first home...it was cream-white stucco feeling, it seemed to be faded with dark red trim, there was the outdoor court yard where the outdoor shower was, small steps to the back or kitchen door. Gray concrete and cinder block wall protected us from the alley. Beyond was a small block of small wooden beach houses with lazy beachside gardens. People seemed to live there. I walked to school. My dog, Puschund, would walk with me everywhere. He was stout, black and tan. He was run over on the Boulevard by my school. Perhaps he was looking for me. They did not tell me for some time...as I had pneumonia twice, perhaps three times. I was the rag doll and the tin soldier there...from asthma, the fog, and perhaps second hand smoke from Daddy.

Peter Raven
The first home I remember living in was a three-story (the lower story a garage) brick house half way up a hill in San Francisco. It was on former dunes, so the back yard was very sandy. My grandfather kept a cage with canaries there, and bred them, and liked to grow fuchsias, which did beautifully in that climate. We sometimes grew vegetables. I had a nice room on the third floor. There was a flower bin built-in in the kitchen, and a former coal-burning furnace in the basement. A horse-drawn wagon came by outside, selling vegetables and offering to sharpen our knives. Golden Gate Park was two and a half blocks away, filled with trees and flowers, museums, an inviting place. It makes me feel happy to think of it!

Patricia Raven
248 Tranquil Avenue. Yes, that is the real street name. And tranquil it was. But what can I remember of a house that we lived in before I was six years old? Things I haven't thought of in decades. Ours was a small, elegant brick house, with white trim and a wide, welcoming tile porch across the middle. At the bottom of the hill, we gained the rain from everyone else's gardens to maintain a magnificent row of water-loving boxwoods along the front. It was a one-story house then, made larger now by others to have a second floor master suite in the former attic.

The house had large windows reaching from the floor to the ceiling. I could see out even if I was sitting on the floor playing. There was one bright window on the sunny side of the dining room. It was there that the maid, Georgia, would put her ironing board when no one else was home. She would enjoy the light on her work and the view from the window into a quiet suburban neighborhood, watching for my younger brother Ted to come home from school. Georgia would make me Campbell's tomato soup and grilled cheese sandwiches for lunch. I'm still fond of them together.

Laura Friedman
It was a suburban tract home, which my mother hated for the sameness of it. They added on a family room, beautiful and cozy, which my first grade class visited en masse (of course back then we walked), when it was under construction. Across the street was a, I believe, 7th Day Adventist structure (was it an orphanage?) that was torn down to make room for a new development. The developer wanted to build apartments; University City said no; he said, if you don't let me build apartments, I'll sell the land to a black developer. Which he did. So we lived across the street from the first black families ever to move to University City and witnessed integration first hand.

It had a big yard, which my father tended (reluctantly) and a big garden along the back drive, which my mother tended (lovingly). It was painted dark red. It was not in the trendy or cool neighborhoods (those were closer to the university), but it was a place our friends liked to hang out. It was on a corner, the anchor of a circular lane. We played ball in the street. Carolyn and I drove by there not too long ago and the house, now, looks too small, and the trees, too big. I wouldn't have recognized it from a picture.

Dan Picus
My first home that I remember living in was a small tract home in a town called Loves Park, just north of Rockford. We lived there for a year while my parents were building what would be our family home for all the time I lived in Rockford. Most of all what I remember of the time I lived in the Loves Park house was going to Nursery School at Mrs. Beal's Play School. I can't remember much of anything of the interior of the house. My sister Miriam was born while we lived in the Loves Park house. I do remember going at least once a week to visit the house we were building on Old Orchard Road. Old Orchard was a former apple orchard and built on a very steep hill. Our backyard was a huge hill and there was the most humongous pile of dirt in the backyard that was great fun to climb.

Ken Kousky
The first home I remember was in Detroit but what I recall are events rather than anything about the house really. When Kathy was born, Dr. Rice and his wife came over and cared for us and he brought me a Bat Masterson cane and gun. There was a TV show at the time with the theme song, "he wore a cane, and derby hat, they called him Bat, Bat Masterson" and that's about all I remember other than a party at one of the neighbors. The next house we had was in Rolla, Missouri at Ft. Leonard Woods.

Two things stand out. First, these were two-story apartments with three or four units in each building. In the bathroom there was a medicine cabinet, which opened behind a mirror and there was a slit in which to drop old razors. If Butch Risler, the guy next door, opened his cabinet we could look through the crack and see each other. It was a secret passage where we could even pass notes. The second noteworthy feature were the big oil tanks in front of the houses – they were oval shapes if you looked at them from the front and must have held 100 or more gallons of heating oil. They were in pairs between the front doors of the units. We would sit on top of them like they were horses and ride around the west, mostly fighting Indians, I think.

Sharon Kousky
The first home I grew up in was a house that my parents built in the early 1950's. It is more structurally sound than most houses built today. It is a ranch with 3 bedrooms, a bathroom, a kitchen, a living room, a family room with a fireplace and a full basement divided into a work area for my dad, a bathroom, a laundry room, a storage room and a living area. It is all brick and because it was built so well, I remember always being warm and cozy. We had a large yard and always had a vegetable garden and lots of flowers.

Urbanities

"The main responsibility of city planning and design should be to develop—insofar as public policy and action can do so—cities that are congenial places for this great range of unofficial plans, ideas, and opportunities to flourish, along with the flourishing of public enterprises."
 —Jane Jacobs,
  <u>The Death and Life of Great American Cities</u>

"The shape of a city
Changes more quickly, alas! than the heart of a mortal."
 —Baudelaire

Civic Spirit

In other words,
> if poetry cannot attain the truth then it cannot attain the concept of justice which the city needs to flourish.

The Monitoring Monitored City.
> Forcing an entity into a representation as a possible root of violence.

'Hori-zoning' the City
> A new method for constructing the endlessly fascinating personality of a city.

>> The last type of agent that Aristotle lists as needing friendship is the city. This is the friendship of alliance. It is akin to the type of friendship that applies to all of humanity for it is another way that individuals or cities are essentially connected. This type of thinking leads one to think about how individuals or cities are "bound" or "held" together. However, the friendship between cities is not at all a natural type of friendship. In fact, it is an almost entirely political form of friendship.

By "political" I mean that the friendship between cities need not be motivated by anything other than the urge to secure power (considered broadly) for the city. It is an entirely contingent form of friendship. But, of course, the major difference between this friendship and the others is that it applies to cities and not individuals. Obviously, this was a trend in the Greek tradition: to think of the individual in terms of the polis and vice versa. Plato makes this trend explicit when he attempts to figure out how a person could be just by using the analogy of figuring out how a city could be just. Plato then takes attributes that apply to the city and applies them to the individual. Aristotle does the opposite. He notes a quality of the individual (friendship) and applies it to the city. This reverses the metaphor and the issue of scale (i.e. from big to small in Plato whereas from small to big in Aristotle). But this type of move should be seen as quite typical of Aristotle who saw concrete particulars (small things) as the basis for all thought (a big thing).

The friendship found between cities demonstrates that Aristotle's conception of friendship is far broader than our modern conception of it. Today we might say that a city was friendly towards another city (its adverbial nature calls attention to the fact that it is a secondary usage of 'friendship'), or was in a coalition or an alliance with another city, but we would not say that two cities were friends. We reserve the designation of friendship for individuals, which makes sense, since in the modern era, our conception of the individual is much more robust than it was in Aristotle's time.

The 'good' now frustrates conceptually,
no expectation for resolution:
a whirlpool before the absolute city.
By 'steam' I meant the impotent spit of motivation.

A Community's[6] Habitat

The radical poem of place[7] is almost wordless

---

[6] A community
is a group of diverse individuals
who either represent themselves
as being in some essential
way connected and possibly homogenous
    or
who are represented as being connected and homogenous.

Therefore,
there is always a tension
between the individuals
and the representation
of them as homogenous group;
there is always a tension
between presentation and representation.

[7] The problem of being a native
keeps coming back
and standing in front of me,
it is a native question.

How many times
do you have to come back
to be called a native?
The sun is native to my existence.
It keeps coming back,
though it is surely wanderlust.

How many meetings
must you attend
before you can speak?
How many meetings

And just as much, almost passionless,
Almost just a setting for violence
Almost just a setting for gathering social change.

'til your mouth stays put?
How many meetings
'til your interests
align with the interests
of the people who stay put?

But, alas, all of these questions
are native themselves
and thus keep coming back,
spiraling back home.

The native never leaves
and in this way,
is never seen speaking,
and in this way,
is thought of as mute, silent,
and in this way,
is seen as not being able to change.

a.

Joke in the Form of a Song about My Hometown

St. Louie Louie
It's just hooey
You have to show me.

St. Louie Louie
Ohh we gotta go
Back to the hotel
To have an affair
On the carousel.

Down and out
On the river deep.
New Orleans here we go,
Mispronunciations
And happy dapper clams
In our dumb dumb hands.

St. Louie Louie
It's just pooey pooey
For some kingsmen fratboys
Looking for a manger
Under the gateway to the fine fine west.

b.

Cambridge, Massachusetts

I've been looking for David Mamet in Harvard Square
because he's famous and a literary guidebook
said I could find him there
between sets of overly posturing breakdancers.

It doesn't really matter who David Mamet is,
whether he elegantly composes sandwiches at Au Bon Pain
or instead hocks slightly damaged Harvard tee-shirts
to sad yet proud parents.

Either way he is constantly sealing a deal
using an abstract gritty language
that keeps my ears puckered,
listening breathlessly baited
for who is selling what to whom.

Perhaps it's the baseball cap that tips me off.
I must have seen him wearing it before,
maybe on a dust jacket beside a quotation
saying that all the dialogue
is as he remembered it growing up

and in this way he is my Julia Child
cooking simple peasant dishes
he knew the tastes of
before the names.

c.

Moab, Utah

The queue for the breakfast buffet
continues to get longer: a half hour
and then 45 minutes. Salty meat
and dry eggs have always made
people want to stand in lines;
waiting for lodge-sponsored activities:
the nightly rodeo with the perfectly timed
tumble (the hat rolling to within an inch
of the crowd, every night!),
and the after dinner chuck wagon
rumbling up the buttery buffet trout,
and the hour long nag walks,
and the dances and the bolo ties:
It's awful and hokey, but wonderful
in a way, that people can still pretend to believe
that the world is still like this.
I heard a man in red flannel say,
or wish I heard him say:
"I just feel so good being here.
It just feels so authentic; I feel a real
connection to the old west here."
Maybe the old west was
always shrouded in hokiness,
maybe it's Buffalo Bills all the way down,
maybe we're closer to the old west than we think.
The line to get in on the buffet finally thins out.

Presumably some of the buffeters have moseyed
on over to the general store
to buy a five dollar role of John Wayne toilet paper,
or a four dollar shaker of cretaceous salt,
or a tee-shirt you can color in yourself,
or a pastel mug bearing a depiction of
a Native-American woman holding a feather
and the words "we can be whatever we
give ourselves the power to be,"
or any of 8 varieties of shot glass from Southwestern Utah,
and, of course, there are the ubiquitous collector's spoons
        culminating in a proof of
                the authenticity
                of any way of life.

d.

Commun(ity)ication

Measured lengths of silk laying equally
on a chair of nice dimensions. "Who said

'nice'?" I did—authority speaking for community—
doors speaking for an entrance of guests;

unexpected objects set upon a minimalist's stage.
Oddly enough, we all agree, it was what we needed.

Why not couple illusions with a stone
attached with a yellow string to a pillar?

"At least community." Hats off, socialize.
A young boy at a desk adding it wrong.

Hats off, community. A picture of how it seeks
to become—flourished organic

from some rainy root in the season of trust.
Why not? At least a string attaches.

Reinsurance Haikus on Shaky Ground

1.

care limitation
X X X X X X X
affords premium

2.

X X X X X
non-payment of premium
liability

3.

processed for lesser
of depreciated cost
or replacement charge

4.

unforeseen event
in consideration of
monthly bill, where fault

5.

X X X X X
subrogation injury
X X X X X

6.

X X X X X
certificate to evi-
dence self insurance

7.

currently rated
coverage open perils
exclusionary

8.

written to cover
losses, risk transfers requi
re hidden knowledge

9.

hedge with definite
homogeneous exposure
X X X X X

10.

(add police report
if crime involved) (attach in
voices to receive)

11.

IT IS A FRAUDULENT INSURANCE ACT FOR A PERSON TO KNOWINGLY OR WILLFULLY MAKE ANY FALSE OR FRAUDULENT STATEMENT OR REPRESENTATION IN OR WITH REFERENCE TO ANY APPLICATION FOR INSURANCE; OR PRESENT AN INSURER, OR CAUSE TO BE PRESENTED TO AN INSURER, DOCUMENTATION OR A WRITTEN OR ORAL STATEMENT THAT IS MADE IN SUPPORT OF A CLAIM AND THAT IS MADE WITH KNOWLEDGE THAT THE DOCUMENTATION OR STATEMENT CONTAINS FALSE OR MISLEADING INFORMATION CONCERNING A MATTER MATERIAL TO THE CLAIM. THE COMMISSION OF A FRAUDULENT INSURANCE ACT IS A CRIME AND MAY SUBJECT A PERSON CONVICTED OF COMMITTING SUCH ACT TO CRIMINAL AND CIVIL PENALTIES.

Major Artery

Bubbles lift through initials scraped in concrete.
Smokestacks pollute, gripping borrowed wedding sheet.

There is nothing new, though businesses open
    and shutter on this corner every year.

    1.
This was where we stood when we said
At first you see merely lines
And then finally your eyes click into the structure

Lifting
But doesn't prevent saying things
In the urgent, exactly, every corner

Thinking down, they elevated us
Without distractions:
I was here, made that change.

Mimic of the grid, but at another level
The work of horses drags one man's pen
Towards obvious distinction, subversion of the small

And yet, your apocalypse team roots in the soil;
Microbes, but no familiar signs
What if I wrote a letter to congress?

2.
We lived here, a real dump
Lifting the spirit of man, only in the distance
The trees of street names always left burning
Hard or soft
Thinking across the city

And if you sweep the other
Saying one thing past another
Finally neither claims order

If direction
Slips through
Unmarked absences

Swear it was on this corner
Where the new road starts out of the old road
When I was young, but now can't

Remember who they were
To revert: this underside
Car to flip, first violence
Until the notes stopped piling
In the excess of the grid
Burnt off on getaway tires

Gun as waved like flag
Dramatically, compositionally interesting
Nobody thought he would hurt anyone
But if he was going to

It had to be on this corner
"…hands…faces…to the ground…else…dead…"

The good Samaritan dutifully played his role
Heroism dispensed
Subsequently shot twice in the face

However as interested, windows sure as shape
Glancing outward
This splattered occasion

Just as chalk on a street is a man
        After he has spoken
Just as the ink of an idea is a city
        Before it has spoken

3.

The mercy of entrance, that other building
Its caveat blooming
Noticed ferment   For meant
Shots you take in the dark
Because you've been there before
Under the remembered stood standing

Instead of these wanton doors
Blisters burst
This new subdivision
Never formulated
Save for the fact that it exists

It flirts with your roof
Falling individually
Whatever is caught is wrenched from the hand
Dirt saves each dream
Dirt and its other, another
As though in a mixture of rooftops we could be steeples.

Without Structure   i
                                                              n
all is loitering if you   d
                               e   t
don't own anything   any fallen, any time: could be me h
e   e   e
v   not really about the structure
intrinsic worth   s   a
c   style of architecture is beside b
e   m   s
             u   t
who am I to say what to spend   r
     f   t w   r   a
                to cold, you must bring them in   c
                r   j   t
                t   e
                h   c
                                 nothing but net
                t   hovel
                o   you have the right
                                               n o
                p   k   that
                around
                s   refers to the worst off people   posh
                s   t
                       e
                       r mines
         absence   of traditions
                    did their marketing

Margin Patrol

```
g
i                       b
v                       u
ethics of restriction   to create a standardized testing
n             e                         regime  e
              w   t                             n
f   labor         o                             d
r      should    r                              s
e      also     e   c
e       be     g    r                           t
        free  u     o                       owards
t       to   l      s                           e
r      move  a      s            exclusion      t
and open the  t                                 e
d      borders i    attached to office          r
e              o                                m
               n                                i
               s    to effect                   n
                                        of    these
             alone, for the prospect of money  hated
                l         r                    e   walls
                w         a     to send back to
                a         c     good neighbors   s
                y         t            make      h
                s         i       good fences   a
                          c                     p
        favoring one group  e of the foreigner  over another
```

88

Herd Instinct

> *in a crowd, people pour like molecules*
> *expanding and breaking apart,*
> *streaming in random directions,*
> *flowing around (or through) obstacles,*
> *but there is no overall coherent*
> *motion.*

When alone I effortlessly move steadily, one foot by one,
Avoiding both running into people and groping them,
But it seems that these days I am always together.

Blocking our chances,
Possibility's traffic jam.
You know how we act when we're the masses.

> …of public/private spaces (i.e. malls, airports, urban centers, suburban streets, etc.), a castaway, you do not necessarily know anyone else in the setting, and you recognize that you have no connection to the people around. You feel alone, though there are many people around. You realize that emotionally, spiritually and intellectually you are alone and that physically you are not alone. What do you do then? You can either act as if you are in your own private space and appear to be crazy and acknowledge the

fact that you have no connection to the crowd, or you can acknowledge the crowd and buy into the illusion that you do have a connection with the crowd.

The madman and the genius both act as if every space is their private space.

> What do I do? How do I act? When I am best I act as if I have realized that I am alone in the crowd, but I also act as if I still wish to make connections with its individuals. When I am worst I am ridiculously self-conscious for the pleasure of others. I always realize later that no one really cares about my self-consciousness; few are watching.

Panicked heat, faster jams building
Pressures capable of bending steel doors
And breaking monumental statues,

Tragically ignoring alternative exits,
But widening the halls just slows us
At the next bottleneck.

Housing Court Sonnet

> "That's his stock in trade — always the victim."

Ailments caused, you are the landlord, supposed
To fix heater's sputter and shower's mold.
"I will sue, I will sue" leaves the door closed.
In countersuit the case will never fold.

Serial litigator, but whose eyes
Are truth, whose eyes could be firm as the facts?
Renters' pathologically pressed ties
Exploit housing bureau's official cracks.

Extortion via court to avoid rent.
"Rent-stabilized guest, yes, you forgot
To mention the cash you reap off each tenant."
All goodwill of guest and host has been shot.

Who will prevail in bureaucratic woe
Is unclear as who will throw the first blow.

Boston Zoning Commission

    Wednesday March 7th, 2007
"to remove one height limit on this block"

where's my paperwork? notoriety's wisdom
when you are whispered, triumphantly
model, straight up; places drawn
against connection, fired off email
have you read this thing?

few little pieces, before inspection
snapped, always been home, then
they get sweet military contracts?
wasn't connected, respondent, said not
true, from his office, detainment

proponent will submit the amendment
could have said quietly late
map amendment & text amendment
extending interim period, essentially covered
the entire downtown area, removed

allows planned development areas, if
anyone opposes, questioning by commission's
same members, before you, in
spite of what you did
unfortunately, no new residential development

competitiveness, as a region, still
best served by mass transit
to alleviate the height limit
more demand for higher offices
surprised by differences tracked, premium

office space in greater demand
than cheap office space, strategies
for downtown growth, suburban congestion
will only become worse, insoluble:
vibrancy will be pulled inward

towards what you decide today won't
remove any other control layer
merely hopefully incent construction, variation
in scale as historical record
booms and busts, spontaneous notions

reemphasized through better planning, legibly
forcing issues of how we
get there, distant skyline lump
permitting work but not grace
underlying significance reflected in congregation

on those commutes, regionally would
get off, destinations outside study
area, new vehicular expeditions, over
existing motions, where you
are in a relationship with core values

Taking the 'People' Out of the City

100. INTRODUCTION

The Phoenix urban renewal plan follows from two earlier studies done for the City of Phoenix. The first was a 1997 City Center plan. The 1997 Center City plan focused on the redevelopment of an area bounded and roughly by Main, Bear Creek, Sixth, and Oak as a new "Town Center" for Phoenix. The 1997 study provided design visions for mixed use developments in center city Phoenix, but did not include recommendations on implementation. To further the 1997 effort, Phoenix undertook a market and implementation study in 2001. That study provided information on the market potential for development in the center city area of Phoenix, recommendations on capital improvements needed to promote the development vision for center city, and suggested long and short-range financing strategies. The financing strategy included a brief renewal feasibility study. This renewal plan and report incorporates and builds upon key components of the 1997 and 2001 studies.

The Phoenix Urban Renewal plan consists of a Part One - Text and a Part Two - Exhibits. The Phoenix City Council acts as the Urban Renewal Agency for the City of Phoenix, Oregon.

This plan has been prepared pursuant to Oregon Revised Statutes (ORS) Chapter 457, the Oregon Constitution, and applicable laws and ordinances of the State of Oregon and City of Phoenix respectively. Any such applicable laws and ordinances are made a part of this plan, whether expressly referred to in the text or not.

94

This Urban R n wa   an f r th   h nix Urban R n wa Ar a was a r v d by th City C unci   f th City f h nix n ___ by rdinanc N . ___.

200. CITIZ N ARTICI ATI N

This r n wa   an was d v   d in a s ri s f six ub ic m tings. Th m tings w r c nduct d by a citiz ns urban r n wa advis ry c mmitt , a int d by th may r and City C unci . M ting t ics inc ud d basic inf rmati n n urban r n wa and tax incr m nt financing, d v   m nt f r j ct g a s and bj ctiv s, d v   m nt f a ist f r j ct activiti s, and a th ugh r vi w f th r v nu s, c sts, and tax im acts f carrying   ut th   r j ct.

Th h nix anning C mmissi n m t t r vi w th   an n August___ 2005. Th h nix City C unci sch du d a ub ic h aring n ad ti n f this   an n August _____ , 2005. Additi na n tic n City C unci ad ti n f th   an was r vid d, as r quir d by RS 457.120.

This   an inc ud s and curr nt y utsid th c r rat imits f h nix. As r quir d by RS 457.105, this   an was a r v d by th Jacks n C unty C mmissi n, by r s uti n dat d August _____, 2005

Fair Housing

>Title VIII of the Civil Rights Act of 1968 (Fair Housing Act), as amended, prohibits discrimination in the sale, rental, and financing of dwellings, and in other housing-related transactions, based on race, color, national origin, religion, sex, familial status (including children under the age of 18 living with parents of legal custodians, pregnant women, and people securing custody of children under the age of 18), and handicap (disability).

"Integration is mentioned in the Congressional Record as a reason for the Fair Housing Act of 1968,"
says Fred Underwood, spokesman for the National Association of Realtors.

INTEGRATE

ASSIMILATE

CLARIFY

If Craigslist has to monitor all of its ads, it'll surely go under.

"not just worried about its financial future,
    but the service it provides.
I mean, the potential of the Internet
is not unlocked by buying a book from Amazon,
but by bringing people together…"

Gathers us through a range of literacy indicators:
Media, Cultural, Financial, Old-Style, Scientific, etc.
    (but to be able to read, to understand,
        is not to become the same)

    Argument: Internet sites are "community-
    moderated commons" not newspapers.

Section 230 of the Communications Decency Act (1995): "No provider or user of an interactive computer service shall be treated as the publisher or speaker of any information provided by another information content provider."
    …resources used to sort…
"…the newly protected classes have proven significant sources…"
    over the "clash with me" ad,
    but I gotta be able to decide who lives with me,
        who shares my bed.
    There have to be limits:
        exemptions for both
(1) a single family home rented by the owner
        or

> (2) *dwellings intended to be occupied by four or less families,*
> *provided the* owner *is also an occupant…*

***

> Will present properties to CLIENT in full compliance
> by presenting "equal access to housing of their choice."
> The beautiful counterpoised with the political.
>
> Deconstructing the myth of the projects
> through the lens and sensuous hypotheses
> of our own heterogeneous racial complexion.

***

You have to think that discriminating
>   by gender some is okay
>   or to need the same…

The knowledge *of*
and the knowledge *needed*
intersect in the state's knowledge regime
($100 laptop for every global citizen)

> "What people have not grasped is that the Internet will change everything," the CEO of Cisco Systems stated in 1998. "The Internet will change how people live, work, play and learn…. And it will have every bit as much impact on society as the Industrial Revolution. It

will promote globalization at an incredible pace. But instead of happening over 100 years, like the Industrial Revolution, it will happen over 7 years…"

…the subject is seen from *the side* of his race, class, gender, or neighborhood. That is, his silhouette is viewed through that lens so that the law-enforcement officer can prevent crimes from occurring. Profiling has an inverse relationship with knowledge from torture. It is the use of generalized knowledge, as opposed to the acquisition of particular knowledge. To profile is to use the generalized (or schematic) knowledge in order to either prevent a future crime or to catch a criminal in the commission of such a crime…

Im(em)minent Domain:

"Is that when a house is just about to happen to you?"
      (Not-So-Primitive Appropriation by The Man)

        Is it
     To jut, threatening...
Being near to pass
       Or is it
          Proximity to
       Distinguished: (used of persons)
Standing above others, attainment of imposing height
          Or is it
             Perhaps merely all in the mind?

       Specters of envisioned space.
What is your paradigm for development?[8]
     Myth of the 'natural.'[9]

       When modifiers cease to matter:
    If they've forced us to sell our houses
To subsidize development
           (condos, retail shops, restaurants, and a

---

[8] Remember, however, that urban development increases the amount of impervious surface area, which increases the speed of run-off and prevents infiltration of water into the earth.

[9] Fake to what?
Let's not talk about fake.
Let's talk about mediation.

> hotel, half of whose rooms Pfizer
> promised to permanently fill)
> Merely to generate higher tax revenues
> To satiate insatiable coffers   then this sphere
Where we come together to care for one another will
Cynically flip with every vacant toss.[10]

> To remove the gaze of trees
> In order to haul necessary materials
> Acknowledging the public kernel
> In every private door, slammed.[11]

> > Yet, no bridge in sight, no park to part the hair
> >   Doesn't
> > Want to build a highway through the property
> >   Doesn't
> > Suffer from blight
> >   Doesn't
> > Want to bring all the citizens together

---

[10] Justice Stevens, writing for the court's majority in Kelo et al. v. City of New London et al: "The city has carefully formulated an economic development plan that it believes will provide appreciable benefits to the community, including … new jobs and increased tax revenue."

[11] John Locke, <u>Two Treatises of Government</u>, Chapter 5, Section 27, "Though the earth, and all inferior creatures, be common to all men, yet every man has a property in his own person: this no body has any right to but himself. The labor of his body, and the work of his hands, we may say, are properly his. Whatsoever then he removes out of the state that nature hath provided, and left it in, he hath mixed his labor with, and joined to it something that is his own, and thereby makes it his property."

> For a deliberative democracy day.
>   Merely, each bad neighborhood
> Replaced by the next to worst…[12]

    Public "use"
        Traded for
    Public "benefit"

My inner libertarian would scream:
    "Property rights are absolute and natural."[13]
    Reduction of humans to essences,
  This one to that one…
Equations swing like monkeys across the political spectrum,
Although trump changes in each conversation.
Fortunately, hopefully, monopolies occur
W/o crossover dominance.

Yet,   <tangent> If they offered me
$10 to travel naked and unescorted
Through the city carrying the cash

---

[12] pissedoffwhitemen from Mosier, Oregon wrote on January 27th 2006: "Where does Ginsberg live (she looks like a bag lady)? I heard her house is so overgrown with weeds and in such disrepair that they want the property condemned because of all the rats it attracts.

You liberals need to clean up yer yards.
Both Souter and Ginsberg live in dumps.
Filthy, stinking dumpholes."

[13] "[N]or shall private property be taken for public use, without just compensation." U. S. Constitution, Fifth Amendment

                    I'd probably do it.
The trick, however,
Is determining when a regulation becomes a taking.

A Couple of Facts

If a couple facts determine the whole history of this place
then a couple of facts are infinitely divisible.

The thing is you wake up
Not knowing what you're talking about.
You haven't necessarily been born where you live.
Your parents haven't necessarily been born where you live.
Therefore, your connection to the land is tenuous.
You were born too late.
You might feel you have
no right to speak about where you live.
It's perhaps an important feeling to have
but it's equally important to get past it:
to say, as much as you can
I do live here:
this is my neighborhood.

On June 30th 2008
we settled on a 2 bedroom/2 bath 1,080 sq. ft. unit (#332)
at Union Row at 2125 14th St. NW Washington DC, 20009.

Because exposed ductwork is the crown molding of our generation.

When I said we were buying
I knew no one else we knew would have made the decision we made:
not gentrified enough, too gentrified.
You're gentrifying; too modern.
No porch, wrong neighborhood.
No yard, wrong school district.
Hidden: too black   (nobody actually thought this
                        but might have thought
                        that somebody else
                        might have thought that;
                        we charge others to
                        believe our beliefs for us).

But we knew it was the right decision for us:
absolutely expressing
who we were at that precise moment:
a perfect purchase.

This was not my father's Oldsmobile.

The Flats: the natural heaviness of I Beams
is contrasted
with man's lifting lightness.

Where We Live
As
Per
Administrative
Analysis:

2002 Single Member District   SMD02 1b04
2008 Voting Precinct   Precinct 22
ANC   ANC 1b
Neighborhood Cluster   Cluster 3
Ward   Ward 1

This is Me
Statistically
Speaking

Carrying, manifesting imagination, will, & cash:

> "Located at 14th and V Streets, NW, The Flats at Union Row is an urban oasis of condominiums with the neighborhood vibe built right in featuring every fine finish and detail including European-inspired kitchen design with granite countertops and stainless steel appliances and sleek and stylish baths with oversized tile and innovative fixtures amidst a vibrant streetscape of shops and cafes, a unique setting among the rhythm and revival of U Street."

To raise steel no man could carry, to grip generators; these are the functions of a crane, but how?
    Base bolted
    mast connected
    slewing unit atop

    and then horizontally, finally
    the jib to haul.

Finally, the engineering works, ingenuity: counter weights
    (gentrification
        +
    tradition).

In the city
everything moves
in the city.
It's not a good idea
to mess with the dynamism
of the city.

No, we only came twice to this neighborhood, but it really resonated with us.

The arc of a neighborhood is not equally proportioned. There is an unknown peak somewhere within.

Unfortunately, the seller is unwilling to negotiate very much on the price for fear that such a move would negatively impact the price of similar units. There is still so much to sell. However, the seller would be willing to cover a significant portion of the closing costs. Although this closing cost credit will be recorded in the sale it will not appear as the final sale price; that's the important point for the seller.

The payment of real estate agents: at the end, after the deal has been completed (therefore, undulations of cash, not a steady gig). If a potential client doesn't end up actually buying on a house-hunting foray the broker leading the expedition will not get paid (no cost to non-buyers). Therefore, clients who actually purchase subsidize showing properties to those who do not buy. Another method (not ours) for paying real estate agents would be to charge clients up front (this would erode the distinction between potential and actual clients).

Time period: 7-10 years.
By that point it'll just be our neighborhood
or we'll sell.

I mean if what you're saying is
you have to have abandoned buildings
for community
I think that's crazy.
In that case, I'm just fine with gentrification.
      However,
any urban architectural feature
comes with something else
namely with what surrounds
with what is seen in the distance
and more will come
more will be seen in the distance
more will block your view in every direction
that more is *development encourages development.*
Even if yours didn't scrape another's from the earth
even if it's environmentally and neighbor friendly
what it urges is more, anything that is more
and that more
might not be
so ethically positioned.

The photographs in our building present our neighborhood's diversity. I guess they're supposed to make you feel both a part of the community and proud of it. They work for me: the diversity they present is relatively easy to swallow.

One print particularly catches my eye:
G. Byron Peck's mural of Duke Ellington
on the True Reformer Building

>sidelines, makes a mayor
>of entertainment.

A jowly Ellington, elderly on brick
collar upturned, masterfully guides the neighborhood

>"letting the dissonant voices
>of each musician play against each other"

to form an American whole, a community of multiplicity

>"Sure, on the weekends it was the 'Black Broadway,' and that's what everyone wants to hear about, but the rest of the time it was our neighborhood, where we came together."
>—A longtime resident

You're always supposed to trust a longtime resident.

How the Mode of Transport Alters Life Above

I think we can take our bikes in the metro during non-peak hours, but we'll have to take them down the elevator by H&R Block.

First, I read that the Columbia Heights Metro
        (the stop one beyond mine) opened in 2001.
Second, it turned out that that was incorrect.
Third, it actually opened in 1999.
Fourth, I assumed that meant that
        the entire green line opened in 1999
        which would have meant that
Fifth, our stop, the U Street/African-American Civil War Memorial/Cardozo Station
        would have opened in 1999
        which would have meant that
Sixth, development patterns in the area
        would have radically changed that year
        but
Seventh, I was wrong about that
        because
Eighth, it actually opened in 1991.
        Thus,
Ninth, this neighborhood
        has had 17 years to soak in public transport.

Zipcar has lately been disappointing. But we'll still use it. How else could we get to IKEA?

Those brands, and our acceptance of them, place us, but not firmly.

RESERVED:
Tuesday, August 5th, 2008
10 AM
Scion xB Bonita
Wagon—4 doors, 4 seatbelts

I know this car has been marketed just for me, but I'm not buying it, so I'll eat that marketing up: "Scion is branding by as many noncorporate methods as possible," explains Jeri Yoshizu, a Scion promotions manager.

As Rob Walker writes, "[U]nlike a Converse or a PBR, Scion wasn't a brand whose meaning originated with consumers and was subsequently amped or nurtured by a company. This time, the 'collaboration' was built into the brand right from the beginning."

But it's okay, using a Zipcar Scion means that I'm part of the movement, but that I can maintain my cred. That's exactly where marketers need to be able to place you.

      Onward,
We arrive at 10. It's not there. A phone call.

"Let's see; it looks like the street spot reserved for Zipcar was taken when the last member returned the car. Sometimes that happens. If it does the member can call us and tell us where the car is."

"So, where is it?"

"Let's see. It looks like they parked it four cars down on Chapin."

It's actually eight cars up, but we get it and head for the large stores in the distance.

      Carsharing is
psychologically different from driving your own car. When you own it you pay all the costs at different times, on different schedules.

Driving a Zipcar you pay all the costs
(save for the environmental and societal ones)
of driving
up front.   It's expensive.

We need a jar to put the savings of not owning a car in so that we don't feel extravagant renting one.

They pay the gas, but prices are rising, theirs as well. As Chadwick Matlin reports in *Slate* (July 11, 2008, at 7:45 AM ET): "Because the gas fee is wrapped into the overall rate you pay when you use a Zipcar, the only way the company can compensate for rising gas prices is by hiking the total cost."

No untangling means the tangle must be raised all together; even explanation does not remove a knot.

There's supposed to be a Zipcar (or "hourly rental car" as our condo docs call it) in our building's parking lot, but it's not there. We ask the real estate agent about it, she says that that'll be up to the condo board to take care of once it takes over. Okay. But then we start thinking about it and realize that given the security features of parking in our building it would be nearly impossible to have a Zipcar there. You'd have to allow strangers to come in both to the building and also the garage unless Zipcar would just rent to residents of the Flats, but that doesn't seem likely; would that even be legal?

Returning from the big box stores the plan was (as it usually is) for me to take the stuff through the door on W and up to our condo while Carolyn parks the car.

But when Carolyn came back home she looked as if something had happened to her, as if something had been taken out of her, at least for the day.

It turned out that someone else was in the Zipcar reserved spot when Carolyn was trying to return it, but that person was still in her car.

"I said, real politely, like she didn't know, 'excuse me ma'am, this is a Zipcar spot.'

She looked at me and rolled up her window. Then she turned away."

The woman was shoving her face with donuts. She might have weighed 500 pounds. Her son was in the back. She was black.

Our neighborhood was supposed to have something utopia in it, something past race. And race wasn't exactly a proxy for her situation, but there is no way that it would be overlooked.

"Finally, I caught her eye again and she rolled her window down and that's when I realized that she was really crazy because she just started spewing at me about how I wouldn't intimidate her into giving up her spot. And I felt so sad for her son.

Finally, I realized I couldn't reason with her and when I saw a police car I started to wave him down: she drove off."

In the midst of the confusing thick, the questions retreat, though they cannot survive without a healthy tax base.

How do we pour that foundation?

As Sarah Nassauer reports for the Wall Street Journal (June 19, 2008; Page D1): "As car-sharing companies have enjoyed skyrocketing growth in recent years, several state and city governments have ruled that car-sharing companies need to charge their members rental-car tax...

...Car-sharing companies argue that they shouldn't be required to pay rental-car taxes because their concept—members renting cars for short periods of time from parking spots close to their home—reduces the number of cars on the road, eases parking and traffic problems and gets people to drive fewer miles."

Luckily, DC doesn't tax car share programs rental-car taxes. Tourists should subsidize the local; I'm just saying

there are a lot of problems;   a lot of problems in this world.

Driving through Tenleytown; suburban but not deep.
Still, a Metro. Carolyn says she might like
to live here
later
like
in 10 years.
That's the date of the future.
I can't picture it.
It's not very urban or diverse.
Well, we'll argue about it later
but
all that could change.
Arguments could untangle themselves
before they even begin.

Harry Wardman (April 11, 1872–March 18, 1938): The Art of Development

NeitherBuilders Nor Dealers Are AreAlarmed
AreAlarmed AreAlarmed
                                              operations
will   construct hundreds of dwellings
            thefact that owners have come to
            torealize toreaze torealize realizethat
            speculative buyers arc arcpractically
            aropraccatly   arepractically
            practicallythe only buyers on the
            mar market market market —
            ketand that nothing is to be
            gained gainedby gainedby gainedi
            byi holding property pr proper at
            high high prices with withthe
            withthe the view of disposing it to
            individual individualbuyers buyers
keeps constructing
operations are breaking all records

in   various
sections of the city: porches on solid foundations

still marketed by realtors to the
next generation of speculative buyers

blewupandweresavedbythegovernment

Seasons of Development

There is a tree in a strange dilapidated
Triangular building across the street.
The tree is not near
But it is something I look at.
I look within the strange triangular building
Because it has no roof. It is all part
Of the jumbled interest. It is fall.
The tree's leaves are looking dried out.
I don't know what kind of tree it is.
I can't get close enough. But
These will be that tree's last leaves.
Soon there will be a new building
Where its relatively old arms have hung.
It's kind of sad to lose the leaves
But I'm excited about all the new stores
And their new things that I will buy.

raisedrazedraisedraze
draisedrazedraisedraz
edraisedrazedraisedra
edraisedrazedraisedra
zedraisedrazedraisedr
azedraisedrazedraised
razedraisedrazedraise
drazedraisedrazedrais
edrazedraisedrazedrai
sedrazedraisedrazedra

A Family Tree of First Homes (Part 3)
My Generation

Daryl McQuinn

The first home I remember living in was on Ladd Avenue in Edwardsville. It was a one-story house painted pink with three bedrooms and one bath. My dad built a garage and a large screened-in back porch. My fondest memory of that house is sitting in front of the heater duct on a cold winter morning letting the duct blow inside my bath robe and fill it with hot air. I had my own room, which was red and white, and the window looked out into the back yard where my parents had planted two trees for my brother and me.

Elizabeth Raven McQuinn

The first house I remember living in was in Menlo Park, California, on Robin Way. I think it was 200 Robin Way, and the house was blue, if I recall, or maybe gray. It was a one-story house with an attached garage that was set back from the road, and it was on a corner lot. There were calla lilies growing alongside the house, and in the backyard we had an artichoke bush. When you walked in, you were in the living room, with the bedrooms to the right through an archway into a hall, and the kitchen to the left towards the back of the house.

Here are things I remember happening there: I remember learning to ride a bicycle with training wheels with my grandfather in the backyard. I remember Daddy walking in from work and hugging his knees and looking up at his belt. I remember going from there to nursery school, which I adored. I remember sleeping in the top bunk bed and having these great dreams of being a fire chief and of waking up with jewels and crowns overflowing my dresser drawers. Alice had her tonsils out while we lived there and she got to sleep in the living room on a sofa sleeper and was given popsicles (jealous!). I remember my sixth birthday party that my mother threw for me, and that she always kept Licorice Allsorts on the counter in a glass canister. I remember driving home from visiting grandmother and granddaddy in San Francisco, and pretending to be asleep every time so that Daddy would carry me inside. He also brought home our first television there, quite astounding, and bought a new blue car, which I at one point managed to coast into the street by myself (my mother came running out and rescued it and me). We would fairly often go to dinner at A&W Root Beer, which had a fireplace and was just past a car dealer with those flags you always see at car dealers. Alice and I would order "Teen Burgers" and feel mighty special.

Alice Raven
Pomona, California, 1963. We lived in a rabbit warren of identical one-story apartments with flat roofs. The living room was a rectangle with a long sofa against the right wall and a stereo on the left wall. The bathroom was straight back from the living room. I can't remember any other rooms. It was always very sunny outside and a little gloomy inside. The apartment had a definite 50s feel. Daddy told me that we were evicted later for letting it get too messy. I don't remember messy, more sparse actually. My very first memory is coming out of the apartment with my mother on the way to the laundry room. Two kids were playing with a little red wagon and I asked if I could play with them: no. One day I wandered

away from the apartment (I was about 3) and went across a busy street to a supermarket. A man was stacking gum into a giant pyramid and handed me a piece. Next thing I remember, I was being spanked by my mother on the sofa, and the gum fell out of my mouth onto the carpet.

Katie Raven
In a way it was beautiful, in the middle of Eden, flowers always were in bloom. My first home was taller than any other—brick on top of brick all the way up, higher than even the ivy could climb. My first home was also larger than any other—larger than the four of us. Asian art on the walls, oriental rugs on the floor, we were growing up in a Missouri that no other Missourian had seen. In the morning, we would look out the kitchen window over the head of our Great Dane and hurriedly ask if we were taking the brown or the yellow car, then we would run out the door on our way to Episcopalian school. We were not Episcopalian. Out back, we would sled down the ivy colored hill, or in another season, swim in the goldfish pond. Browns and deep blues and the browns in my room were ancient furniture and wallpaper of a maze of trees and I had brown sheets. We ate pizza on the orange floor and stayed up later than we were allowed to watching jaws, blue jaws.

Francis Raven
I grew up in the Director's House at the Missouri Botanical Garden (at 2361 Tower Grove, St. Louis MO 63110), a Tudor mansion (though a small one) built in 1914 on about an acre of land, which encompasses a pond (behind which was my dandelion garden), an enormous oak (up which the one-handed

man who trimmed the tree and with whom I was fascinated would climb) which rather recently died (in the past ten years), a large vegetable garden, and a pair of cast-iron gates (one of which was electronic, but which could be squeezed through if you tried hard enough, a trick we soon taught the pizza man) beside which are the graves of several dogs, mainly Great Danes. Since I have known the house for almost 30 years it's hard to remember when certain events occurred, although sometimes it seems that my whole life occurred there.

Carolyn Kousky
I only lived in the first home I remember until I was about seven. The house was red brick, with a driveway on the right, at the end of which were a couple raspberry bushes. One time we found a box turtle under the bushes and kept it as a pet for a while. When you walked into the house there was a living room on the left. I played with my imaginary friend, Amy, in that room. On the right when you walked in the house was our playroom. We had a train set and a record player on which I'd listen to Bambi. We also had a fish tank with a fish that jumped out of the tank several times. It scared me to see it thrashing on the floor. The kitchen was behind the dining room, which was behind the living room. We had a large wooden table in the kitchen. At one birthday party I had make-your-own-sandwiches around that table. I put Jell-O on mine and thought that was very creative of me. In the kitchen there was a door to the backyard. We had a swing set. Upstairs my sister and I shared a bedroom. We each had a twin bed. Across the hall was our parents' room. One time I got scared in the middle of the night and crawled in next to my dad. I swear monsters

popped up around the bed. There were block parties on the street in front of our house sometimes. At one summer block party my friend showed me how to catch lightning bugs and pull the lit part off their bodies and stick it on your ear like an earring. I thought it was gross but wanted earrings like her anyway. I learned to ride a two-wheel bike on that street. Sometimes we'd take the street further into the neighborhood on bike rides as a family. We'd sing "Downtown" by Petula Clark and "Leaning on a Lamp Post" by Herman's Hermits. Many years later I walked back by the house with Francis. It was so much smaller than I remembered. And oddly comforting.

Rebecca Kousky
We had a secret passageway in our first house. Carolyn and I could slip into the closet from our shared bedroom and end up in our parent's room. What new parents would choose such a house with two young girls? We moved before I was 5 so the only other thing I remember was that I broke a sprinkler in our backyard one summer.

A New Kind of Bomb in the City

Explosion without the sound
An expansion of every surface
Mugs, lamps, walls, books, ladders

Splits bricks
All around the so-called swelling mass
Engorging all the air around

The fireball slows below the speed of sound
Shockwave 'breaks away'
From its relative constant

Pocket seams finally burst
Fish dies
Dries out in Brooklyn summer

Foregrounding clean lines of a leader's saxophone
Constantly bending procedures, brow beating foreign civilians
Territorial inflation

Depends upon the height of impact
Airburst for minimum fallout
High altitude to break the most glass

And always
After the beauty
The flames

Resources

MixTape for that Funky Building

Artist	Title	Duration
Paul Simon	Homeless	3:48
The Pogues	Sunnyside of the Street	2:43
Bravo Silva	City I Love You	4:14
Architecture in Helsinki	City Calm Down	2:49
Modest Mouse	Paper Thin Walls	3:01
The Decembrists	Here I Dreamt I Was An Architect	4:31
Talking Heads	Don't Worry About the Government	3:00
Postal Service	This Place is a Prison	3:55
Ben Kweller	My Apartment	3:57
Joni Mitchell	Big Yellow Taxi	2:15
David Rovics	More Gardens Song	3:12
Phish	Bouncing Around the Room	4:08
Lucinda Williams	Changed the Locks	3:44
Red Hot Chili Peppers	Under the Bridge	4:24
	Total Mix Duration:	49:41

An Open Source Anthology of Architecture Poems

(Listed alphabetically to avoid making decisions.)

Ammons, A. R.; The City Limits
http://plagiarist.com/poetry/2994/

Apollinaire, Guillaume; Mirabeau Bridge
http://plagiarist.com/poetry/7958/

Baudelaire, Charles; The Swan
http://www.poetry-archive.com/b/the_swan.html

Bukowski, Charles; The House
http://plagiarist.com/poetry/191/

Carson, Anne; The Life of Towns
http://www.nyu.edu/classes/neimark/carson.html

Cavafy, C.P.; The Polis
http://www.flashpointmag.com/polis.htm

Crane, Hart; To Brooklyn Bridge
http://plagiarist.com/poetry/3710/

cummings, e.e.; my love is building a building
http://plagiarist.com/poetry/310/

Dickinson, Emily; THE PROPS assist the house
http://www.bartleby.com/113/5026.html

Frost, Robert; Mending Wall
http://www.poets.org/viewmedia.php/prmMID/15719

Gunn, Thom; A Map of the City
http://www.poemhunter.com/p/m/poem.asp?poem=1947918

Heaney, Seamus; An Architect
http://plagiarist.com/poetry/9245/

Larkin, Philip; The Building
http://plagiarist.com/poetry/4873/

Merrill, James; An Urban Convalescence (audio)
http://archive.salon.com/audio/poetry/2001/03/14/merrill/index.html

O'Hara, Frank; A City Winter
http://www.poemhunter.com/p/m/poem.asp?poet=8255&poem=105848

Perec, Georges; On the difficulty of imagining an ideal city
http://www.thingsmagazine.net/text/t8/perec.htm

Pound, Ezra; In a Station of the Metro
http://www.bartleby.com/104/106.html

Robertson, Lisa; Wooden Houses
http://www.jacketmagazine.com/27/robe.html

Sandburg, Carl; Chicago
http://www.poets.org/viewmedia.php/prmMID/15262

Sandburg, Carl; Skyscraper
http://plagiarist.com/poetry/4746/

Strand, Mark; The Tunnel
http://www.poemhunter.com/p/m/poem.asp?poet=8391&poem=1207134

Swensen, Cole; The Invention of Streetlights
http://www.poets.org/viewmedia.php/prmMID/16693

Vincent, Stephen; Walking Theory
http://www.mipoesias.com/2006/vincent.html

Whitman, Walt; Mannahatta
http://www.bartleby.com/142/161.html

Whitman, Walt; Once I Pass'd Through a Populous City
http://www.bartleby.com/142/26.html

References
[Websites]

A Digital Archive of American Architecture
http://www.bc.edu/bc_org/avp/cas/fnart/fa267/

International Architecture Database
http://www.archinform.net/index.htm

American Institute of Architects
http://www.aia.org

The Great Buildings Collection
http://www.greatbuildings.com/

Illustrated Architectural Dictionary
http://freenet.buffalo.edu/bah/a/DCTNRY/vocab.html

Architecture News
http://archibot.com/

Architecture Forum
http://www.designcommunity.com/discussion.html

Blogs

A Daily Dose of Architecture
http://archidose.blogspot.com/

Architecture Sketches
http://architecturesketches.blogspot.com/

Architectnophilia
http://architechnophilia.blogspot.com/

Architecture and Morality
http://www.architectureandmorality.blogspot.com/

Magazines

Metropolis
http://www.metropolismag.com/cda/

Dwell
http://www.dwell.com/

Architectural Record
http://archrecord.construction.com/

Books

Abrams, Janet and Peter Hall, eds., Else/Where: Mapping — New Cartographies of Networks and Territories. (University of Minnesota Press, 2006).

Alexander, Christopher. A Pattern Language. (Oxford University Press, 1977).

Bachelard, Gaston. The Poetics of Space. (Beacon Press, 1994).

Benjamin, Walter. The Arcades Project. (Belknap Press, 2002).

Botton, Alain de. The Architecture of Happiness. (Hamish Hamilton Ltd, 2006).

Certeau, Michel de. The Practice of Everyday Life. (University of California Press, 1984).

Debord, Guy. The Society of the Spectacle. (Zone Books, 1995).

Giedion, Siegfried. Space, Time and Architecture: The Growth of a New Tradition, Fifth Revised and Enlarged Edition. (Harvard University Press, 2003).

Harries, Karsten. The Ethical Function of Architecture. (MIT Press,1998).

Jacobs, Jane. The Death and Life of Great American Cities. (Vintage; Reissue edition, 1992).

LeGates, Richard T. and Frederic Stout, eds. The City Reader. (Routledge, 1999).

Koolhaas, Rem, Bruce Mau, and Hans Werlemann. S M L XL. (Monacelli Press, 1997).

Lefebvre, Henri. The Production of Space. (Blackwell Publishing, 1991).

Macaulay, David. Underground. (Houghton Mifflin, 1976).

Morsiani, Paola and Trevor Smith, Andrea Zittel: Critical Space. (Prestel Publishing, 2005).

Rand, Ayn. The Fountainhead. (Signet, Centennial Edition, 1996).

Robertson, Lisa. Occasional Work and 7 Walks from the Office for Soft Architecture. (Clear Cut Press, 2003).

Sadler, Simon. The Situationist City. (MIT Press, 1999).

Stoner, Jill, ed. Poems for Architects. (William Stout Architectural Books, 2001).

Tuan, Yi-Fu. Space and Place: The Perspective of Experience. (University of Minnesota Press, 2001).

Acknowledgements

Some of the poems in this volume were originally published, sometimes in a greatly different form, in *Vibrant Gray, Letterbox, Stylus, Sub-Lit, Indefinite Space, Switchback, The Hidden City Quarterly, Crit, Square Table, Philadelphia Stories, Buffalo Carp, Edgz,* and in the chapbook, *Judging Our Allies* (Grey Book Press, 2009). Thanks so much to the editors for first seeing these poems into print.

Bio

Francis Raven's books include *Provisions* (Interbirth, 2009), *5-Haifun: Of Being Divisible* (Blue Lion Books, 2008), *Shifting the Question More Complicated* (Otoliths, 2007), *Taste: Gastronomic Poems* (Blazevox 2005) and the novel, *Inverted Curvatures* (Spuyten Duyvil, 2005). Francis lives in Washington, DC. You can view more of his work at: www.ravensaesthetica.com.

www.ingramcontent.com/pod-product-compliance
Lightning Source LLC
Chambersburg PA
CBHW070458100426
42743CB00010B/1671